Cursive
HANDWRITING WORKBOOK

Awesome Cursive Writing Practice
Book for Kids and Teens

Capital & Lowercase Letters, Words and
Sentences with Fun Jokes & Riddles
(Cursive Writing Workbook)

FOR
KIDS AND
TEENS

Clever Kiddo

Copyright (c) Clever Kiddo Books

Guided Practice

a

a

Unguided Practice

a

a

a

a

a

a

a

a

a

a

a

Animal

Abracadabra

Aficionado

Unguided Practice - Practice writing the words yourself

Guided Practice

Unguided Practice

Babushka

Bamboo e

Blabbermouth

Baboon

Bombastic

Bonkers

Unguided Practice - Practice writing the words yourself

Caboodle

Cackatoo

Cunundrum

Unguided Practice - Practice writing the words yourself

D D D D D D D D D D D

d d d d d d d d d d d

D D D D D D D D D D D

d d d d d d d d d d d

D

d

D

d

D

d

D

d

D

d

D

d

Digerido

Dillydally

Doodad

Unguided Practice - Practice writing the words yourself

Epiphany

Extraterrestial

Unguided Practice - Practice writing the words yourself

Fiasco

Flamingo

Fricassee

Unguided Practice - Practice writing the words yourself

Guided Practice

Unguided Practice

Gizmo

Guru

Goosebump

Unguided Practice - Practice writing the words yourself

Heebie-jeebie

Heyday

Horsefeathers

Unguided Practice - Practice writing the words yourself

Guided Practice

Unguided Practice

Infinite

Incredulous

Interloper

Unguided Practice - Practice writing the words yourself

Guided Practice

Unguided Practice

Juggernaut

Jibber-Jabber

Jawbreaker

Unguided Practice - Practice writing the words yourself

K

k

K

k

K

k

K

k

K

k

K

k

K

k

Kerfuffle

Kaleidoscope

Kaput

Unguided Practice - Practice writing the words yourself

$\mathscr{L}$

ℓ

$\mathscr{L}$

ℓ

$\mathscr{L}$

ℓ

$\mathscr{L}$

ℓ

$\mathscr{L}$

ℓ

$\mathscr{L}$

ℓ

$\mathscr{L}$

ℓ

Loggerhead

Log-or-rhe-a

LogJam

Unguided Practice - Practice writing the words yourself

m m m m m m m m m m m

m m m m m m m m m m m

m m m m m m m m m m m

m m m m m m m m m m m

m

m

m

m

m

m

m

m

m

m

m

m

Machinations

Mastermind

Muckety-muck

Unguided Practice - Practice writing the words yourself

Guided Practice

n

n

Unguided Practice

n

n

n

n

n

n

n

n

n

n

n

Guided Practice

Nomenclature

Noodge

Namby-pamby

Unguided Practice - Practice writing the words yourself

Guided Practice

Unguided Practice

Outlandish

Oxymoron

Outfox

Unguided Practice - Practice writing the words yourself

p *p* *p* *p* *p* *p* *p* *p* *p* *p* *p*

p *p* *p* *p* *p* *p* *p* *p* *p* *p* *p*

p *p* *p* *p* *p* *p* *p* *p* *p* *p* *p*

Unguided Practice

p

p

p

p

p

p

p

p

p

p

p

p

p

Piffle

Phantonym

Potpourri

Unguided Practice - Practice writing the words yourself

Q Q Q Q Q Q Q Q Q Q Q Q Q Q Q

q q q q q q q q q q q q q q q

Q Q Q Q Q Q Q Q Q Q Q Q Q Q Q

q q q q q q q q q q q q q q q

Unguided Practice

Q

q

Q

q

Q

q

Q

q

Q

q

Q

q

Q

q

Quirky

Quiblile

Quicksticks

Unguided Practice - Practice writing the words yourself

R

r

R

r

R

r

R

r

R

r

R

r

R

r

Rubberneck

Riffraff

Razzle-dazzle

Unguided Practice - Practice writing the words yourself

Guided Practice

Unguided Practice

Swizzlestick

Switcheroo

Superlicious

Unguided Practice - Practice writing the words yourself

𝒯

𝓍

𝒯

𝓍

𝒯

𝓍

𝒯

𝓍

𝒯

𝓍

𝒯

𝓍

𝒯

𝓍

Teepee

Topsie-Turvy

Terriffic

Unguided Practice - Practice writing the words yourself

$\mathcal{U}$

w

$\mathcal{U}$

u

$\mathcal{U}$

u

$\mathcal{U}$

u

$\mathcal{U}$

u

$\mathcal{U}$

u

$\mathcal{U}$

u

Ululation

Umlaut

Umpteen

Unguided Practice - Practice writing the words yourself

$\mathcal{V}$

$\mathcal{V}$

$\mathcal{N}$

$\mathcal{V}$

$\mathcal{N}$

$\mathcal{V}$

$\mathcal{N}$

$\mathcal{V}$

$\mathcal{N}$

$\mathcal{V}$

$\mathcal{N}$

$\mathcal{V}$

$\mathcal{N}$

$\mathcal{V}$

$\mathcal{N}$

Vertigo

Verisimilitude

Virtuoso

Unguided Practice - Practice writing the words yourself

𝒲

𝓌

𝒲

𝓌

𝒲

𝓌

𝒲

𝓌

𝒲

𝓌

𝒲

𝓌

𝒲

𝓌

Wigman

Wishy-Washy

Wonky

Unguided Practice - Practice writing the words yourself

χ

x

χ

x

χ

x

χ

x

χ

x

χ

x

χ

x

χ

x

Xylophone

$\mathcal{Y}$

$\mathcal{Y}$

Unguided Practice

$\mathcal{Y}$

$\mathcal{Y}$

$\mathcal{Y}$

$\mathcal{Y}$

$\mathcal{Y}$

$\mathcal{Y}$

$\mathcal{Y}$

$\mathcal{Y}$

$\mathcal{Y}$

$\mathcal{Y}$

$\mathcal{Y}$

$\mathcal{Y}$

$\mathcal{Y}$

Yellow-belly

Yo-yo

Yokel

Unguided Practice - Practice writing the words yourself

Sentence Writing Practice - Jokes and Riddles

What did the duck say

to the comedian?

You quack me up.

Unguided Practice - Practice writing the words yourself

How do all oceans say

hello to each other?

They wave!

Unguided Practice - Practice writing the words yourself

Sentence Writing Practice - Jokes and Riddles

What do you call a
Santa that doesn't move?
Santa Pause!

Unguided Practice - Practice writing the words yourself

Why did the banana
go to the doctor?
Because he wasn't peeling very well!

Unguided Practice - Practice writing the words yourself

Sentence Writing Practice - Jokes and Riddles

What do you call a
cheese that isn't yours?
Nacho cheese!

Unguided Practice - Practice writing the words yourself

Why couldn't the pirate
play cards?
Because he was standing on the deck!

Unguided Practice - Practice writing the words yourself

Sentence Writing Practice - Jokes and Riddles

Knock, knock.

Who's there?

Cows go.

Cows go who?

No, cows go MOO!

Unguided Practice - Practice writing the words yourself

How do you make

an octopus laugh?

With ten-tickles!

Unguided Practice - Practice writing the words yourself

Sentence Writing Practice - Jokes and Riddles

What did the nose say
to the finger?
Quit picking on me!

Unguided Practice - Practice writing the words yourself

What did one wall say
to the other wall?
I'll meet you at the corner!

Unguided Practice - Practice writing the words yourself

Sentence Writing Practice - Jokes and Riddles

What do you call a
fake noodle?
An impasta.

Unguided Practice - Practice writing the words yourself

Knock, knock.
Who's there?
Who!
Who who?
That's what the owl says.

Unguided Practice - Practice writing the words yourself

Sentence Writing Practice - Jokes and Riddles

What stays in the corner
yet can travel all over the world?
A stamp.

Unguided Practice - Practice writing the words yourself

Knock, knock.
Who's there?
Ya.
Ya who?
Wow, I'm excited to see you too!

Unguided Practice - Practice writing the words yourself

Sentence Writing Practice - Jokes and Riddles

Why can't Elsa have balloons?

Because she will let it go.

Unguided Practice - Practice writing the words yourself

Knock, knock.

Who's there?

Atch.

Atch who?

Bless you!

Unguided Practice - Practice writing the words yourself

Sentence Writing Practice - Jokes and Riddles

What do you call a
funny mountain?
Hill-arious.

Unguided Practice - Practice writing the words yourself

Knock, knock.
Who's there?
Boo!
Boo! who?
Don't cry. It's just me.

Unguided Practice - Practice writing the words yourself

Sentence Writing Practice - Jokes and Riddles

Why didn't the orange
win the race?
It ran out of juice.

Unguided Practice - Practice writing the words yourself

Knock, knock.
Who's there?
Figs
Figs who?
Figs the doorbell, it's broken!

Unguided Practice - Practice writing the words yourself

Sentence Writing Practice - Jokes and Riddles

Knock, knock.

Who's there?

Olive

Olive who?

Olive there next door to you.

Unguided Practice - Practice writing the words yourself

What sounds do porcupines

make when they hug?

Ouch!

Unguided Practice - Practice writing the words yourself

Sentence Writing Practice - Jokes and Riddles

What has a face and two hands
but no arms or legs?
A clock.

Unguided Practice - Practice writing the words yourself

Knock, knock.
Who's there?
Nobel
Nobel who?
No bell, that's why I knocked!

Unguided Practice - Practice writing the words yourself

Sentence Writing Practice - Jokes and Riddles

Why did the man put his
money in the freezer?
He wanted cold hard cash!

Unguided Practice - Practice writing the words yourself

I have all the knowledge you have.
But I am small as your fist that your
hands can hold me. Who am I?
I'm your brain!

Unguided Practice - Practice writing the words yourself

Sentence Writing Practice - Jokes and Riddles

What has to be broken

before you can use it?

An egg.

Unguided Practice - Practice writing the words yourself

What did one toilet say to the other?

You look flushed.

Unguided Practice - Practice writing the words yourself

Sentence Writing Practice - Jokes and Riddles

Knock, knock.

Who's there?

Orange.

Orange who?

Orange you glad to see me?

Unguided Practice - Practice writing the words yourself

Why are ghost bad liars?

Because you can see right through them.

Unguided Practice - Practice writing the words yourself

Sentence Writing Practice - Jokes and Riddles

What occurs once in a minute, twice in a moment and never in one thousand years? The letter M.

Unguided Practice - Practice writing the words yourself

Why did the dinosaur cross the road? Because the chicken wasn't born yet.

Unguided Practice - Practice writing the words yourself

Sentence Writing Practice - Jokes and Riddles

Where does the Friday
come before Thursday?
In the dictionary.

Unguided Practice - Practice writing the words yourself

What kind of award
did the dentist receive?
A little plaque.

Unguided Practice - Practice writing the words yourself

Sentence Writing Practice - Jokes and Riddles

Find me! I start with 'P' and end with 'E',
but I have thousand of letters. Who am I?
Post Office.

Unguided Practice - Practice writing the words yourself

Why did the skeleton
go to the dance?
He had nobody to dance with.

Unguided Practice - Practice writing the words yourself

Sentence Writing Practice - Jokes and Riddles

Everyone in the world needs it. They generously give it. but never take it. Then what is it?

Advice.

Unguided Practice - Practice writing the words yourself

How do you fix a cracked pumpkin? With a pumpkin patch.

Unguided Practice - Practice writing the words yourself

Sentence Writing Practice - Jokes and Riddles

A boy and an engineer were fishing. The boy is the son of the engineer but engineer is not the father of the boy. Then who is the engineer? The engineer is the boy's mother.

Unguided Practice - Practice writing the words yourself

What is the word that is spelled incorrectly in all dictionaries? Incorrectly.

Unguided Practice - Practice writing the words yourself

Sentence Writing Practice - Jokes and Riddles

Why did Jhonny throw the clock
out of the window?
Because he wanted to see time fly.

Unguided Practice - Practice writing the words yourself

How do you make the number
one disappear?
Add the letter G and its "gone."

Unguided Practice - Practice writing the words yourself

Sentence Writing Practice - Jokes and Riddles

Knock, knock.

Who's there?

Broccoli

Broccoli who?

Broccoli doesn't have a last name, silly.

Unguided Practice - Practice writing the words yourself

Which flower talks the most?

Tulips, of course, because they

have two lips.

Unguided Practice - Practice writing the words yourself

Sentence Writing Practice - Jokes and Riddles

Knock, knock.

Who's there?

I am.

I am who?

You don't know who you are?

Unguided Practice - Practice writing the words yourself

Why did the girl smear

peanut butter on the road?

To go with the traffic jam!

Unguided Practice - Practice writing the words yourself

Sentence Writing Practice - Jokes and Riddles

Knock, knock.

Who's there?

Ketchup.

Ketchup who?

Ketchup with me and I'll tell you!

Unguided Practice - Practice writing the words yourself

What did 0 say to 8?

Nice belt!

Unguided Practice - Practice writing the words yourself

Sentence Writing Practice - Jokes and Riddles

Knock, knock.

Who's there?

Lettuce.

Lettuce who?

Lettuce in, it's freezing out here!

Unguided Practice - Practice writing the words yourself

What do you get when you cross a
snowman and a vampire?

Frostbite!

Unguided Practice - Practice writing the words yourself

Sentence Writing Practice - Jokes and Riddles

Knock, knock.

Who's there?

Ice cream.

Ice cream who?

Ice cream if you don't let me in!

Unguided Practice - Practice writing the words yourself

Why did the vampire get fired

from the blood bank?

He was caught drinking on the job!

Unguided Practice - Practice writing the words yourself

Sentence Writing Practice - Jokes and Riddles

Knock, knock.

Who's there?

Doughnut!

Doughnut who?

Doughnut ask, it's a secret!

Unguided Practice - Practice writing the words yourself

Name four days of the week

that start with the letter "T"?

Tuesday, Thursday, today and tomorrow.

Unguided Practice - Practice writing the words yourself

Sentence Writing Practice - Jokes and Riddles

Knock, knock.

Who's there?

Interrupting pirate.

Interrup... Arrrrrrrrrr!

Unguided Practice - Practice writing the words yourself

What kind of lion never roars?

A dandelion!

Unguided Practice - Practice writing the words yourself

Sentence Writing Practice - Jokes and Riddles

Knock, knock.

Who's there?

Double.

Double who?

W

Unguided Practice - Practice writing the words yourself

Why was 6 afraid of 7?

Because 7, 8, 9.

Unguided Practice - Practice writing the words yourself

Sentence Writing Practice - Jokes and Riddles

Knock, knock.

Who's there?

A broken pencil.

A broken pencil who?

Oh never mind, it's pointless.

Unguided Practice - Practice writing the words yourself

Where do pencils go for vacation?

Pencil-vania.

Unguided Practice - Practice writing the words yourself

Sentence Writing Practice - Jokes and Riddles

Knock, knock.

Who's there?

Wooden shoe.

Wooden shoe who?

Wooden shoe like to hear another joke?

Unguided Practice - Practice writing the words yourself

What has hands but cannot clap?

A clock.

Unguided Practice - Practice writing the words yourself

Sentence Writing Practice - Jokes and Riddles

Knock, knock.

Who's there?

Dishes.

Dishes who?

Dishes a nice place you got here.

Unguided Practice - Practice writing the words yourself

What do elves learn in school?

The elf-abet.

Unguided Practice - Practice writing the words yourself

Sentence Writing Practice - Jokes and Riddles

Knock, knock.

Who's there?

Iva.

Iva who?

I've a sore hand from knocking!

Unguided Practice - Practice writing the words yourself

Why did the boy bring

a ladder to school?

He wanted to go to high-school.

Unguided Practice - Practice writing the words yourself

Sentence Writing Practice - Jokes and Riddles

Will you remember me in 2 minutes?

Yes.

Knock, knock.

Who's there?

Hey, you didn't remember me!

Unguided Practice - Practice writing the words yourself

What do skeletons say before eating?

Bone Appetit!

Unguided Practice - Practice writing the words yourself

Sentence Writing Practice - Jokes and Riddles

What time do you go to the dentist?

At tooth-hurty!

Unguided Practice - Practice writing the words yourself

What gets wetter and wetter

the more it dries?

A towel.

Unguided Practice - Practice writing the words yourself

Blank Practice Pages

Blank Practice Pages

Blank Practice Pages

Blank Practice Pages

Blank Practice Pages

Blank Practice Pages

Blank Practice Pages

Blank Practice Pages

Blank Practice Pages

Blank Practice Pages

Blank Practice Pages

One last thing – we would love to hear
your feedback about this book!

If you found this book enjoyable and useful, we would be
very grateful if you posted a short review on Amazon! Your support
does make a difference and we read every review personally.

If you would like to leave a review, just head on over to this
book's Amazon page and click "Write a customer review."

Thank you for your support!

Made in United States
Orlando, FL
01 September 2022

21801329R00057